Keep Kids Out of Porn

The Governments Intentional Failure

by

Marc Lafond

Publisher: Ingram Spark
(The Ingram Content Group)
1 Ingram Blvd. MS 395
La Vergne, TN 37086
http://www.ingramspark.com

Author: Marc Lafond PhD, MBA

Softcover ISBN: 978-0-9766321-1-5
EPUB ISBN: 9781087934167

Printed in the United States of America

First Edition

Table of Contents

Bill H5414 South Carolina General Assembly

The essence of this work is to offer a solution to the South Carolina Bill H5414 regarding the abuse of children and women in adult entertainment and the dangers of child exposure to online pornography. An innovative approach called OSOMA can be that answer. This approach would minimize the exposure of pornography from the eyes and minds of our children, prohibit child exploitation in pornography, and generate billions of dollars in government revenue. Let our kids grow up in a family environment free from the hazards of online pornography.

Dedication

The dedication of this book is to my brother that was sexually abused as early as nine years old and had no one to help him fight for justice.

Preface

The primary aim of this work is to offer an inventive solution to minimize minors from accessing pornography online, which can destroy their lives. Another fundamental purpose of this work is to examine why the government's actions were negligent in establishing regulations that prohibit child exploitation in pornography. The federal government has taken great strides to create laws that ban child pornography but has failed to cover all the gaps of child abuse because of neglect and lack of moral duty. Last, this work incorporates a plan of action that could bring the government billions of dollars in revenue from online adult entertainment while saving the taxpayers' countless dollars.

Unsubstantiated by scientific research, this work reasons itself upon speculation, deduction, opinion, insight, personal experience, and observation. This leaves an opportunity for academic research to uncover evidence to support or refute its underlying assumptions and conclusions. This publication is not supporting or opposing adult entertainment but renders an alternative to satisfy its dissenters and offer satisfaction for the First Amendment right viewers.

Part I: GACC Exploitation and Deception

Chapter 1: Introduction

Every webpage in adult entertainment should be unconditionally clear of child related content, whether in words or pictures. It is illegal to photograph or video minors engaged in sex or posing nude in inappropriate positions, but why is it still legal in porn to have category names, words, and links that imply children engaging in nudity and sexual activity. Adult entertainment must also seek a better means to deter our minors from gaining access to its hazardous content. Moral citizens demand a drastic change within online pornography to eliminate all aspects of child exploitation and prohibit minors from gaining access.

The government (GOV) passed laws banning online pictures and videos of children engaged in sexual activity and provocative nudity. This was an important first step to reduce child exploitation within online adult entertainment. However, these laws failed to embrace all the areas of child exploitation that are clearly visible within pornography today. The areas unprotected comprise child related words, links, categories, and pictures within webpages containing nudity, sex, and pornography referred to as gray area child content (GACC). GACC also comprises websites that lack pictures and videos but contain children related words, links, and categories that suggest children are engaged in nudity or sexuality within subsequent webpages.

The GOV failed to unearth a better means of protecting our minors from gaining access to online adult entertainment. In today's world of technology, our minors can still gain access to pornography even though households engage in internet blocking practices. South Carolina bill H5414 states that the typical age of minor exposure to pornography is between nine and eleven. Teenagers that engage in porn can develop a misconception about the reality of sex and relationships. Porn can rewire a teenager's brain to think in a distorted manner by corrupting their perception regarding family, marriage, morality, and fidelity. Regulators have neglected to construct a better plan to keep our youth from accessing porn on the internet and the question is why?

Porn has become an uncontrollable multibillion-dollar industry lacking adequate regulation to criminalize and fine website owners for fraud, abuse, and misrepresentation. Porn website owners use GACC freely to attract viewers, optimize inadvertent redirects, label deceptively, and some steer viewers to illegal content. Website owners create categories such as incest, rape, and bestiality that use women and children in an exploitive manner. There is little to no enforcement to stop these website owners from their immoral practices. There needs to be legislative reform to eliminate GACC, block underage access to porn, keep all adult entertainment confined to a secured login portal, and criminalize website owners for abuse, misrepresentation, and deception. We need a strong solution to solve America's porn problem.

The out of sight, out of mind approach (OSOMA) is a method that can provide a solution. OSOMA goal is to augment the current child pornography laws by illegalizing GACC and website owner abuse and fraud while blocking underage access to porn. This approach would use Internet Search Engines (ISE) as the backbone in developing technology inclusive of artificial intelligence to monitor and control porn, while reducing taxpayer costs. In implementing OSOMA, the federal government would generate millions of dollars in annual revenue from fees and duties.

Why use ISE's? These multibillion-dollar ISE firms employ skilled software engineer experts with knowledge in controlling queries within their database of sources that can confine all adult entertainment to a secured login portal. The adult entertainment login portal would require age verification, proof of address (e.g., Utility bill), a onetime application fee, and annual user duties. Under OSOMA, the only entrance for adult entertainment on the internet is through the secured porn portal that would block minor access. With this protection barrier in place, an internet search for topics related to nudity, sex, or pornography would result in zero findings. OSOMA would also introduce new legislation to prohibit website owner abuse and deception and eliminate immoral categories. OSOMA is the answer that would keep the internet a very safe and clean environment for all ages to enjoy the information and knowledge that it possesses. Moral citizens demand a change in how pornography is accessible online. Now is the time for change to protect America from the beast of porn!

Chapter 2: GACC

Gray area child content (GACC) may seem harmless to those that are not active within online adult entertainment. However, child related words, categories, links, and visual depictions are clearly positioned within adult entertainment where millions of aroused viewers are seeking sexual satisfaction. Even the adversaries of porn such as homemakers, devote religious folks, and anti-porn activists have failed to realize GACC destructiveness within online adult entertainment.

The GOV violated their moral and conscientious duty when they failed to seal all the gaps to protect child exploitation within porn. GACC comprise words related to children; child pictures in advertising; child modeling advertisements; pictures of children on modeling login pages; clothed children; naturalist (nude) pictures of children in open content and within advertisements; deceptive website navigation techniques using child pictures or names in baiting schemes; and webpages containing references or hints of children engaged in sexuality. The government (GOV) should have created legislation to prohibit all GACC found within webpages containing nudity, sex, and pornography. Just place nudity, porn, and a gender in any search engines query box with the filter off and the results would yield many links to GACC websites. There is no reason why the GOV has allowed millions of aroused males to encounter children sexually, whether implied or explicit, within pornography.

Porn rewires the brain and weakens one's mental defenses, which leads a viewer into becoming more vulnerable to its content. Deceptive website owners that create GACC within porn attempt to get aroused males interested in younger models. Stimulated neuronal and hormonal activity does not instantaneously stop when viewers come across child content after looking at adult pornography for hours. The environment of porn makes it easy for a viewer to become indifferent and uninhibited about GACC.

Viewers of adult entertainment have the right to enjoy their first amendment rights without running into the temptation of GACC. Adult viewers do not need manipulation by those website owners that play games using children as lures to create sexual excitement. Children are not bait, whether in words or pictures. Yet, our GOV has been doing an extremely poor job at stopping

GACC and even child porn from entering online websites for decades. It is unknown where sources of child porn originate until found, investigated, and disclosed to the public through the news media. Yet, the GOV spends our taxpaying dollars wastefully because they cannot eliminate it from the web.

Moral citizens demand regulation that prohibits child visuals and words from sitting in front of millions of porn viewers that are seeking sexual gratification. We must put a stop to this beast of destruction that seemingly has full GOV approval. Principled parents and religious people would oppose this type of content if they knew it existed. Prolonged engagement in GACC content may lead males into looking at children as sexual objects. Who are the website owners that use children as baiting mechanisms to get sexually aroused males to look at them?

Chapter 3: Porn Category Names

The lack of government (GOV) oversight in matters dealing with pornographic website control has led to lenient, ambiguous and child related categories, links, and words. Some of these questionable gray area child content (GACC) categories comprise teen, young, lolita, and barely legal that imply children within its sexually explicit material. These websites and categories are easily accessible on the internet by conducting a simple word search along with the word porn. Just place nudity, porn, and sex terms in a search engines query box and the result would yield many website links containing GACC. Website owners use GACC because the implication is that aroused adult males will find youth, virginity, and innocence within its contents, which creates a level of excitement.

However, the extensive and uninhibited use of child related categories and names within hundreds of adult websites creates an insensitivity among porn viewers. This is a sad fact. A conditioning effect triggers active porn participants to associate the words teen and young to mean universally legal nudity and sexuality. Mental barriers can easily break down with the repetitive and extensive use of child related words creating total ignorance by the adult viewer.

There are other category names buried within adult porn containing implicit and explicit references to minors. These categories include junior, nymphets, little girls, preteen, young, and youngest, daddy's daughter, tiny, small, and jailbait among others. What are these names doing in adult entertainment in the first place? By their inaction, the GOV seems to approve children's categories in adult porn where millions of pleasure-seeking males are searching. Why has the GOV allowed this to exist?

Conditioned that there is nothing wrong with the category name teen, millions of active porn viewers choose it without a second thought when it shows up on countless sexually explicit websites, links, videos, or pictures. When a viewer clicks on the teen category, they experience models that are eighteen years of age and older. If we look at the true definition of teenager (teen category), we find that the word represents individuals between the ages of 13 to 19. Roughly, 29% of the teenager definition falls within the legal porn age limit whereas 71% of the teenager definition falls outside the legal age limit. Presumably, all models within the teen category are at least 18, but the word teen still implies all teenagers from ages 13 to 19.

Pornography has created an impression in the viewer's mind that anything affiliated with the word teen is sexually legal. So, when the word teen shows up on any adult website, the viewer may perceive it to be perfectly safe and normal to click on. The risk is very apparent in that website owners can bait adult entertainment viewers using the word teen, which can lead them to illegal content. Why are the teen categories within pornographic websites not banned by our GOV when 70% of the teen definition falls outside the legal limits? In its true ethical context, the GOV should have banned the word teen from all websites within pornography.

Porn viewers can choose another category called young to gain instant access to sexually explicit material. The category name young are popular within many pornographic websites. The repetitive and considerable use of young creates a total ignorance and insensitivity by the adult entertainment viewer. The young category, like teen, contains models over eighteen. The website owner's purpose in using this category name could be to lure individuals to view youth, innocence, and virginity.

If we analyze the word young outside of pornography, it refers to an early stage of development in the human life cycle, such as a young child. The standard dictionary definition of young can vary but it relates to youth, child, junior, lolita, adolescent or one that is not mature. So, what do you think is the difference between the category's young, teen, and lolita in porn? Nothing, they all have remarkably similar meanings according to Webster. In looking them up in porn, the meanings attached to these underage words are nudity and explicit sex.

The starting age considered under the standard definition of the word young could be as little as three years old. A viewer can become conditioned and insensitive to the real meaning of the word young because of its commonality within countless pornographic websites. In lacking any respect for the word, viewers strive to uncover the sexual content found under the young category without showing inhibition or restraint. What happens when they come across words of similar meaning like junior, youngest, and lolita buried within porn content? Do they feel the same way? Website owners can lead viewers into illegal content by just using the young word on their websites.

Another category used loosely is the classification called barely legal, which lies at the very base of sexual legitimacy. We can assume that by clicking on this category a viewer enters the land of virgin newbies or those that just lost innocence. If we breakdown this category name, the true meaning becomes interesting. Within a matter of one day, an individual turning from age seventeen to eighteen is now "barely legal" for explicit nudity and sex for the entire world to witness. Think about it. They were illegal the day before, and now they are legal. It is amazing what a difference one day makes.

So, what is in the viewer's mind while surfing the young category on the web, looking for sexual satisfaction? Well, when turning the drinking age did you get excited about turning legal. Therefore, the assumption is that barley legal cause's excitement because the porn viewer experiences the virgin exposed to the world for the time. Ideally, the implied sexual content of this category sits on the edge of legality.

Legislation needs to be created that prevents individuals from displaying nudity and sex on the internet until they reach the age of nineteen but keep the age of eighteen for legal sex. A reason is that many porn vultures' prey on innocent eighteen-year-old girls to become victims for the entire world to experience. Many naive girls have regretted going nude or engaging in sex on the internet at eighteen. We need to change this as a responsible society, and the GOV needs to intervene to take corrective action.

The teen, young, lolita, and barely legal categories in mainstream pornographic sites can condition a person to feel at ease and extremely comfortable when viewing its content. These categories create a level of mental acclimatizing that produces full acceptance in the viewer's mind, thinking it is normal. This mental conditioning generates a thinning risk level that can lead porn followers into taking a lighter approach toward associating all teens, lolita, and youth with legally explicit sex. To further complicate matters, there are porn websites that not only use teen and young categories within the entire web pages but use words like junior, nymphets, little, young and youngest, defloration, daddy's daughter, small, tiny, and jailbait to entice sexually unsatisfied males. A responsible

GOV should reevaluate GACC category names and prevent website owners from using them for adult entertainment, but they do not.

It is illegal to photograph or film nude individuals posing in inappropriate positions under the age of eighteen, but why is it still legal to have category names, words, and links that imply children engaging in nudity and sexual activity. Porn website owners are exploiting children by placing them as category labels, links, and words. They are baiting our children like meat to aroused males. The potential result is that active porn viewers repeatedly coming across these categories become numb or desensitized to the true meaning of child-related words. Could these porn website owners create an impression that child related words are perfectly normal with sexuality? Could these categories generate a desire in the aroused males mind to explore children precariously? These categories could steer a porn viewer into illegal content when luring, baiting, or inadvertent redirection occurs through website owner manipulation.

In recap, pornography has created an impression in the onlooker's unconscious mind that words associated with children are legal and sexual. Porn enthusiasts observing these words time after time again feel extremely comfortable selecting them. This could be a very plausible reason why child porn baiting and luring schemes, using adolescence names, can easily capture the attention of unsuspecting porn viewers. There is something seriously wrong with these category labels that imply children within porn.

The lack of legislation implies that the authorities could not care less about child-related words that appear in countless pornographic websites. Further, by not placing bans on GACC, the GOV is consenting that porn enthusiast should feel perfectly normal selecting these categories. The GOV needs to create legislation banning child words, links, and categories in pornography referencing children to nudity and sexuality.

Chapter 4: The Brain and Porn

In the last chapter, we examined how easy it is for a viewer to select child categories impulsively, because of the standardization and repetitiveness within mainstream pornography. This conditioned acceptance creates indifference or insensitivity regarding the true meaning of child related words frequently appearing like young, teen, lolita, youngest, and "barely legal". However, readily accepting questionable terms is only part of the viewer's total experience. There are other variables that need examination when attempting to comprehend the observer's state of mind during a porn session. Therefore, it is important to dwell within the potential psychological and physiological effects that can take place in a viewer's brain and body when engaging in porn. However, not everyone experiences porn to the same degree, especially when trying to piece together the fine line of addiction.

When a viewer interacts with pornographic material, there takes place a psychological and physiological change in the mind and body. A male watching porn is in a state influenced by hormones, neurological chemicals, and brain electrical activity. The hormone testosterone somehow plays a part in sexual release, drive, and excitement. Dopamine and serotonin are neurotransmitters released within the brain that connects to the feelings of ecstasy, excitement, and the desire for more. Activated norepinephrine, like adrenaline, relates to a person's alertness, motivation level, and mental absorption.

The effect of activated hormones and neurotransmitters results in viewers experiencing an induced high of want, enjoyment, and escape. In this stream of conscious desire, excitement, and exploration, the mind may open to visual and auditory levels of mesmerizing pleasure. Like shots of Morphine or Novocain that can relieve a person from experiencing pain, a porn viewer may want to keep that pleasuring sensation flowing endlessness. The deeper a porn viewer's enjoyment and involvement in streaming porn, the easier it is to accept anything that comes into sight. We can easily observe this from individuals wanting to experience unconventional sides of sexual pleasure.

Not everyone experiences porn in the same manner. However, we can speculate that individuals engaged in porn are at a transformed state of mind when compared to those that are not engaged in porn. For example, there are two people in a room on a hot day. One is thirsty and the other not. We bring a glass of ice water into the room. Which person would want it more, the unsatisfied, or the satisfied individual? The neurotransmitter dopamine somehow creates the desire to want more and more. Dopamine somehow plays a role that keeps gamblers putting coins in a slot machine, looking for the next desired level of satisfaction. The male enthusiast effected by hormones and neurotransmitters may find it hard to stop streaming porn, therefore desiring newer and newer levels of satisfaction.

A porn advocate may find many benefits from streaming adult entertainment. It can provide self-satisfaction, relieve stress, relax an individual's state of mind, rid headaches, moderate blood pressure, normalize desire, help insomnia, spark up a sexual relationship, inhibit prostate cancer to a degree, and refresh the body's mechanisms. It can be a type of therapy. Self-stimulation is the safest form of sex because it avoids sexual transmission of diseases from one partner to another. Some negative benefits from pornography among others are that it can withdraw a person from society, generate depression, destroy intimacy with a partner, and become addictive. Opponents of porn consider it immoral, perverted, destroyer of family values, and nonproductive.

What would you think happens in the brain of teenagers that views porn regularly? Porn can inhibit a teenager's normal mental growth and corrupt their outlook on life right into adulthood. High school students that watch porn regularly may have trouble acquiring knowledge. Porn might create setbacks like impeding a student's motivational level to seek higher levels of education. Because of the psychological and physiological effects that it can have on a teenager's brain and body, porn must be regulated on the internet with restricted access. In confining porn to a login portal, teenagers will have a great difficulty accessing its contents without a User ID and password.

Chapter 5: Porn Website Deception

Selecting a desired location from a navigation bar on a standard website will redirect an individual to the exact location desired. For instance, if "contact" from a drop-down menu on a business website is selected, it would redirect the user to a webpage that contains contact information. When an internet user searches a term within images, the standard protocol upon clicking a picture would cause an enlarged version. However, these expected protocols do not always apply within many adult entertainment websites. Some porn website owners use deceptive tactics in relation to links, words, pictures, and videos that when selected can lead into unintended areas.

Inadvertent redirections occur when a porn viewer clicks on a category, link, picture, or video describing one thing, but a different page unrelated to the desired outcome opens. The viewer plans on heading in one direction and the click leads them into an unintended path. It is important to note that not all links and videos within porn inadvertently misdirect individuals all the time.

Inadvertent redirections can occur with for many reasons. One reason might be that some website owners' direct consumers to their advertiser's webpage for revenue generation. By selecting a video within a web page, they may redirect the viewer to an adult dating site or a paid service. Some website owners have a stake in adult entertainment services, and steering viewers through inadvertent redirects can generate additional revenue. Another reason could be that a video displayed on one website is located elsewhere. For instance, if a watcher clicks on a specific video to watch within a webpage, they will end up on the actual hosting site or even on a sister website. Redirects can also occur within almost any porn page, but more so for webpages containing many GACC links.

Some adult entertainment supporters like to explore less popular websites because of the differentiation in content, reduction in the number of porn stars, and a greater number of natural amateur's performances. Many popular adult entertainment sites have professional female stars that cake their face with makeup and can easily fake their audience. Less popular porn sites may have real amateur actors with natural features and performances that are more authentic.

However, less popular websites may use deceptive links and redirects to a greater degree. For example, if a viewer clicks on the link called young and legal, the link could redirect them to another porn site but not young and legal. If the viewer hits the back page and selects young and legal again, they may end up on yet another website unaffiliated with the original link. Website owners that use these deceptive links are trying to steer people to malware, a different porn site, GACC, or even illegal content.

Another type of deception that can occur in pornographic websites is falsely labeling or creating mystery links or categories, like XXZY1. What does that mean and where does it go? A good deal of porn streaming explorers will take the challenge and click on whatever they encounter. Clicking on these deceptive labels is somewhat like playing the game of what is behind the curtain. These redirects are a game played by the website owners for driving the porn viewer into questionable content.

Porn has become a very uncontrollable industry on the internet with shenanigans going on for years. Some adult websites can keep viewers guessing where they will land when clicking on words, categories, and links. Websites active in inadvertent redirects and mystery links could lead the viewer into pages that contain GACC or even illegal content. Website owners involved in redirects and mystery links should face financial penalties, website closures, and criminal proceedings for falsification, misrepresentation, and deception. Why is GOV enforcement absent to take these websites offline to protect adult entertainment viewers? It makes a person wonder if the GOV allows the abuse and deception within porn websites for some undisclosed reason. Porn has gotten way out of control and needs GOV legislation to step in and make some ethical changes to protect citizen viewers. Citizen porn viewers are taxpayers.

Chapter 6: Children in Adult Entertainment

Website owners that create gray area child content (GACC) webpages in porn are exploiting children. In pushing the limits of the law, some owners strive to create webpages on the edge of legality leaning toward illegality. Just type sex and gender terms in a search engines query box and the result would yield many website links containing GACC. Website owners shrewdly assemble countless pages of GACC related names, links, and categories in attempt to gain the curiosity of their victims. This devil's craft implements inadvertent redirects as one key deceiving technique that steers viewers into questionable areas of porn. The website owner's goals are to drive aroused males into taking an interest in young, teen, lolitas, and even child models. Some website owners even use tricky words, links, and layouts with unsuspecting outcomes. Websites that steer porn viewers to child related content in porn are called child transition pages. Child transition pages also include webpages that contain adult nudity or porn with children in view, either clothed or nude. Why would an ethical website owner use child within porn, either implied or explicit, to capture the interest of sexually aroused males? If a sexually aroused male shifts their interest toward children because of these transition pages, the result could be child sexual objectification (CSO). One definition of CSO is a point where an aroused person views children as sexual objects and desires to experience more pictures and videos.

Some websites contain sexually explicit adult porn content combined with child modeling advertisement. Child modeling websites comprise underage clothed children in various postures. Female child models can appear dolled up, caked in makeup, and dressed in skimpy clothing, which can give an appearance of maturity. Sometimes child models can appear in questionable poses that could be on the edge of enticement. It would only seem rational that the target market for child-modeling sites is media publication firms, movie producers, or even marketing departments of companies. However, child-modeling advertisements positions itself within porn pages that contain explicit adult nudity and sexuality. Child-modeling advertisements are targeting sexually aroused male viewers to become attracted to children.

Child modeling companies even advertise in porn, stating that their website is "absolutely legal". Wow, "absolutely legal" child-models available for sexually aroused adults to experience, enjoy, and peak. Owners of these websites hope that stimulated and interested porn spectators might click on the child-modeling advertisement, enter the website, and possibly become infatuated with the pictures and videos. We can assume that child-modeling sites desire to bait horny males to sign up and receive child pictures for a subscription cost. Child-modeling websites are apparently GOV stamped and approved for adult entertainment.

The bottom line is that child-modeling advertisements in porn entice stimulated male viewers to take an interest in child models as a form of sexual entertainment. Child modeling sites can persuade aroused males to look at children as sexual objects. Without a doubt, child-modeling advertising should be well outside adult entertainment and banned from advertising pictures of children on their website cover pages.

Naturalistic websites comprise pictures and videos of family members in the nude interacting on beaches, private family gatherings, or camps. Nude beach pictures depict adults and children on the sand enjoying the sun and water, which seems very innocent. There are international beaches around the world that allow all family members to strip down bare to get an even tan. However, many nude beaches in the US limit the underage population from taking off all their clothes.

In some naturalist websites, there are pictures and videos of family members showing it all within gatherings at various facilities such as a private campground. They depict both nude adults and nude children engaging in many activities like swimming, body painting, and boating, which is apparently legal. There are also pictures and videos of pageants that contain nude children of all ages, judged by adults as they strut their stuff onstage in front of an audience. It is inconceivable as to the judging criteria used for pageants involving nude children of all ages. Are the pageant administrators looking for a perfect body while getting lustfully excited about nude children?

Some of these naturalist advertisements contain nude pictures of children that are observable through web searches. This does not seem right. Pictures of nude children should not be in open site as a marketing tool to bait aroused males as they stream through porn. For thousands of years adult males had sexual relations with preteens and young teens. Nonetheless, the laws have changed to reflect new standards within our society. Therefore, today's laws must deter naturalistic sites from displaying pictures of children (clothed or nude) to the public when they conduct searches through porn. However, the GOV will not close these sites down for some reason. These pictures should only be available for members after they logon to a naturalist website.

Then there are webpages that contain no pictures or videos but only teen and young related words, categories, icons, and links. The website owner cunningly entices the viewer to select a word or link to uncover expected pictures or videos of young or teen models. When the viewer clicks an icon implying that a teen picture will appear, there are no pictures resulting. Website owners use this format to manipulate and misrepresent their implied intention to the viewer. A viewer clicking on these deceptive links enters webpages upon webpages containing no connection to the original links.

The website owner through their cunning deception may lead the porn viewer into pages containing child words like junior, nymphets, lolita, little boy, little girls, preteen, young and youngest, very-very young, daddy's daughter, tiny, small, incest, rape, jailbait and more. Nothing is stopping websites owners from developing a webpage that contains only words or links that insinuate children engaged in sexual activity. Some mainstream adult websites create child pages to attract males and redirect them to their legal adult sex site. However, some of these webpages might redirect a watcher into illegal porn.

There is also a large traffic flow of male viewers clicking through the young and teen categories within porn. Some website owners create teen and young porn pages filled with pictures. A click of any picture on a page would lead to more legal nude pictures, some with sexual situations. However, slowly the website owner would add one or two clothed underage models combined with legal nude adults as a viewer clicks through more webpages. A subsequent page may even contain a nude child from a naturalistic website. Then at one point, even clicking on a nude adult can lead to webpages filled with questionable words and links insinuating children are engaged in nudity or sex on subsequent webpages.

Another game some website owners create is the third-party trick that plays off of a 18 U.S.C. disclaimer.

Scrolling to the bottom of a page containing nude pictures may display a 18 U.S.C. disclaimer indicating that all models are of legal age. The line underneath it might state something to the effect that they are not responsible for third party content. If a viewer selects a picture within this website, they can be easily redirected to a website containing illegal child content, child models, or pages with links indicating illegal content on subsequent pages. Tricky but an effective way of getting aroused males to look at children.

Immoral website owners use deceptive techniques to attract males in sexual heat by slowing incorporating children into subsequent webpages for baiting purposes. It is surprising the GOV would allow a non-naturalistic website to contain both pictures of legal models engaging in nudity or sexual activity with pictures of naturalistic (nude) young children. There are not any laws prohibiting words or links that insinuate children will be engaging in nudity or sex on succeeding pages.

What is in the porn viewer's mind when they enter a child transition page? While under the influence of porn, a male viewer is excited and aroused, flipping through adult entertainment. Sexually stimulated neurons and hormones do not stop when a viewer comes across child content after looking at explicit adult porn. These mental states and physiological feelings may continue when they run into pictures of children. What happens when the male viewer's brain is stimulated on the sight of clothed or nude child pics found in porn? Acceptance and impaired judgement can easily override reality, leading the porn viewer into leaning toward children as sexual objects. Males that once saw children as non-arousing and innocent could eventually become fixated in a precarious manner.

Child exploitation is clearly a present activity within GACC transition pages. Yet, there is no GOV regulation banning child-modeling sites from advertising within websites containing nudity, sex, or pornography. Additionally, there is not a ban on using the terms "absolutely legal" within child modeling advertisements that can gain an aroused man's interest. There is no legislation banning naturalist children (nude kids) pictures from showing up on non-naturalist's websites. Finally, pageants containing nude children are immoral and legislation should prohibit such open activity. Illegalizing child transition pages will stop millions of aroused males from viewing such content as they stream through porn.

In recap, website owners strive to create content that sits on the edge of legality leaning toward illegality to entice aroused male viewers. Child transition pages bate and persuade male viewers to become sexually curious about children. Potentially, these websites are trying to get viewers to go over the edge into illegality. Why is GOV enforcement absent to take these websites immediately down to protect adult entertainment viewers from this immoral content? Are not viewers taxpayers? Through their inaction, it is apparent the GOV is approving these websites to exist for adult viewer's entertainment.

In lack of legislation prohibiting child transition pages, the GOV is paving the way for the conversion of some sexually aroused active porn viewers into becoming pedophiles, rapists, and murderers. Children talk freely about what they experience every day to their parents. What would someone potentially do that raped a child? Would they allow that child to live? It only takes one addicted porn viewer to rape and kill innocent children due to the influence of child transitional webpages found within pornography.

The GOV is having trouble finding the large list of missing children in America. Some of these missing kids could be the result of child transition pages, GACC, and child porn found within adult entertainment that has influenced some viewers into become predators. Porn can change a viewer's brain and sometimes the wrong way, depending on content that they experience. The GOV does not even have warnings posted in porn to stop or warn viewers about this content. What is this telling us about responsibility?

Chapter 7: GACC and Illegal Porn

Illegal porn could originate from any place in any country. Therefore, it is unknown where sources of child porn originate until found, investigated, and disclosed to the public through the news media and even the court system. We know that there are deceitful and immoral website owners that try to sneak child porn through deceptive webpages, presumably using GACC as a bridge. We also know that the GOV is doing a poor job at eliminating child porn from the web due to the news reports and court cases about people possessing it. If we stop immoral website owners from using GACC within porn, then the entrance of child porn onto the internet could be difficult. Further, making internet search engines (ISE) responsible for enforcing illegal porn content would save taxpayer millions of dollars over time and enhance control.

Porn enthusiasts that have been around long enough know that child porn can mostly comprise fake (doctored) pictures. For instance, a fake picture can show an adult nude body altered to look small with a picture of a child's head planted on top. Fake porn can also comprise children engaged in animated sexual activity. In either case, possessing fake or real child porn is a crime. It is a felony to download these pictures on any devise. The penalty to possess these fake pictures is like that of committing robbery with a loaded pistol. The loaded pistol can kill you; fake child porn cannot. Fake child porn is a murderer's tool that has destroyed human lives through online deception.

Over the years, the GOV has spent millions of taxpayer dollars enforcing child pornography laws and even going to the extent of using methods that are manipulative, unethical, and deceitful to catch violators. For instance, a court case described the GOV using software tools to open the door of home computers to retrieve citizen's private files to uncover illegal child content. In another court case, the GOV managed a website that was uploading and downloading thousands of child porn pictures. In running this porn operation, the GOV allowed steering, baiting, and exploiting children to spark the curiosity among sexually aroused male viewers.

Sexually aroused male viewers deserve their freedom in viewing porn without interference or distractions. Adult entertainment should absolutely be free of any child related content. One reason is that when a person is willfully engaged in porn, there are psychological and physiological changes that take place in the brain and body that causes modifications in perception, acceptance, vulnerability, and judgement. When active porn viewers become enticed, mesmerized, and excited through hormones and triggered neurotransmitters, porn of all types can become very attracting and accepting. The neuronal and hormonal activity does not instantly stop when males come across child content after viewing adult sexually explicit material. GACC is a shear danger to the viewer.

Where are the GOV signs and roadblocks to warn citizens about potential illegal porn sites as they stream through the internet? Nowhere! This makes little sense and concerned citizens wonder why because children are being exploited. Imagine a sixty-five mile an hour road alongside a steep cliff with deep curves. If the GOV did not provide signs to slow drivers down to thirty-five, whose fault is it when someone drives off the cliff and dies? The GOV probably says that it is not our fault. The GOV has not only failed to eliminate child porn from the internet but failed viewers by not posting warning signs within adult entertainment informing citizens of potentially dangerous areas.

The GOV attitude appears to be one sided when it comes to porn. Their actions imply that individuals should not be driving on the porn road in the first place because it is dirty, filthy, and perverted. In fact, the GOV is indirectly saying that you have no rights as a citizen to watch porn and we are going to make it hard by allowing impeding obstacles like child exploitation. It appears that website owners can do as they please without authoritative intervention.

A major problem is that our regulators created laws regarding child porn and some website owners are taking advantage of these laws by playing games with viewers using GACC. GACC has not been illegalized and can be used as a bridge to illegal content. Where does it stop? It clearly appears that the GOV does not have the capability to control illegal porn on the internet. Therefore, a universal plan of attack needs to be in place that stops website deception and promotes full honest transparency between the viewer and the creator of adult entertainment. This plan will stop child exploitation from occurring within adult entertainment.

We know that the developers of fake child porn are deprived individuals with unethical values that seek to destroy human lives. Males for thousands of years engaged freely in sexual relations with preteen and teens, which was very natural and socially acceptable. Today, cunning website owners create content that entices a male's innate nature. Yet, the GOV turns their head to this type of website fraud, deception, and manipulation.

Website owners that redirect viewers to illegal pictures are playing a dangerous game with citizens that are enjoying their First Amendment rights. Sexually aroused males deserve their freedom in viewing porn without interference, distractions, GACC, or redirects. It is just sad to think that there will be many victims in the future falling to corrupt website owners. Some of these future viewers would probably be people that enjoy watching adult entertainment in the privacy of their homes. The games need to stop within adult entertainment. We need a better plan of control and monitoring to allow citizens their rights while impeding our youth from gaining access to porn.

Chapter 8: Taking-Down Men through Porn

This is a true story about a store detective that was always number one when it came to catching shoplifters. The detective's routine was to position himself in an observation post above the ceiling tiles, looking out a two-way mirror. The mirror was in an unobstructed view of two music CD's isles. One day a manager from the store was in a nearby isle close to the store detective's post, but out of sight. He noticed that there was someone shopping in the music isle. He heard a faint voice coming through the ceiling. He listened carefully and the store detective was talking in a low tone, making these statements. Take it, take it, no one's around. Take it, take it, it is ok. Feel good! Hide it, quickly, quickly. Take it and leave swiftly. At that point, it became apparent to the manager why the store detective was successful at catching shoplifters.

Is it possible that active adult entertainment viewers can encounter external influences while streaming porn that may guide their choices? In previous chapters, we discussed the abuse of GACC, the indifference of terminology, hormonal and neurotransmitter activity, website owner abuse, deception, and manipulation. We

40

examined how physiological and psychological factors could impel the viewer into a dopamine state of mind filled with pleasure and want that can lead them into acceptance, vulnerability, and impaired judgement. Yet, another influence can also be present within the environment that can lead the viewer into making decisions about the porn content that they select. These influences can come from outside observers that can use various deceptive tactics to persuade and direct the viewer to make unconscious decisions.

To gain a better understanding of how external influences can steer a porn viewer into inadvertent web content, we will examine this hypothetical example. Let us say that skilled psychological manipulators work on observer teams with the technological capability of watching the internet activity of any citizen. Team members can consist of two or more personnel that work together on any operation. Observer team members have real time access of the viewer's webpages or webpage links as they navigate through the internet. Team members can always visualize the viewer's current webpages or links. Team members also have the capability in reviewing the search history of anyone that views online content.

Let us say team members only focus on a viewer's live porn streaming activity or web links. The team can analyze viewer porn historical data to determine patterns and interests. Could teams implement tactics that can unconsciously influence the viewer's behavior and direct them into choosing certain content? The answer is yes. It is possible to implement strategies that are in the form of verbal suggestion and feeling manipulation that can persuade the viewer into online content desired by the observer teams.

Think about the store detective story. Providing simple suggestions to others can direct their minds to those activities. Whether they act upon those suggestions depends upon many factors. However, using the power of suggestion to persuade someone's mind over a prolong period has a greater impact than just a few brief moments. Ask any experienced salesperson trying to close a big sale over a years' time. Elongated verbal seduction can lead a human being in a direction that they may not have taken if the verbal suggestions were absent. Observer teams trained in the art of verbal suggestion and feeling manipulation can cautiously and slowly over time persuade the mind of the viewer to seek new interests within porn.

Teams of women and men with persuasive and seductive skills can make suggestions within an audible range that can entice, excite, deter, and guide the victim to observer-targeted locations. Suggestions with feelings can pair up to create a new experience for the viewer. It is as if a glamorous female model is pulling a chain around the necks of vulnerable aroused males leading them through sensuality and pleasure. Sissy hypnosis videos found within porn utilize suggestion and visuals that can drive men into becoming transvestites or taking a sexual interest in males. These videos are psychological manipulation tools to get males to accept new behaviors, especially those seeking sexual satisfaction. These videos can turn a straight man into a bisexual or gay man over time. It is surprising that the sissy videos usually contain female voices trying to persuade men to seek a new interest. What is that telling us about the seductiveness of a female voice?

As an observer team member meticulously acquires the daily porn pattern of a viewer, they can start to control their thoughts, behaviors, and movement. It all depends on the susceptibility of the porn viewer. The observer team must be able to maintain one-step ahead of the viewer as if they are simultaneously putting words into their mouth. The observer needs to get to a point where suggesting leads a viewer to act on that recommendation. This persuasion and suggestion process using voice transmitting and listening devices placed near the viewer's location can facilitate success. The teams could even be miles away with planted devices in an audible position to the target victim. Technology can allow teams to cut into radio signals and even SiriusXM that make suggestions to the person while they drive. Succinct suggestions through radio transmission signals can allow the team to have more control over the victim and keep them running.

So, what is stopping observer teams from persuading males to look at GACC and even seek out illegal porn using various techniques after studying their patterns and interests? Moreover, certain catalysts can augment the viewers' experience to make it more satisfying and addicting. Catalysts could be in the form of creating a high-level of excitement along with sexual heat to intensify the viewers' encounter. We already know that suggestive videos like the sissy hypnosis in porn can create feelings of excitement and heat that can attract men. A male in heat can peak a lot quicker when it comes to sexuality. Therefore, the combination of verbal persuasion, sexual heat, physical excitement, innate desire, hormones, and neurotransmitter activity can create an observer-controlled experience that can get viewers hooked on GACC and even illegal content.

Worldwide GOV agency observer teams can take down top tier executives, politicians, wealthy men, or the average person that enjoy watching porn and are susceptible to suggestion. These agencies just need to learn viewer routines and porn interests, slowly and cautiously take control of viewer streaming though suggestion and begin to steer their victims into destruction. A lengthy process, but it can become highly effective.

However, there are elements observer team's needs in place before they can destroy a person by taking away their wealth, self-worth, family, and career. First, the possession of child porn must be a high-level crime where the victim resides. Next, keep all types of GACC legal, which is a bridge or gateway to lead into illegal porn. Then hide fake child porn in areas accessible through GACC and attainable through inadvertent redirects. So, all the teams need to do is get the viewer interested in GACC, psychologically steer them to illegal porn, and make an arrest. The reality is that anyone can fall victim to observer teams if they are vulnerable to suggestion.

Hypothetically, observer teams could even create a website with multiple pages containing GACC words, links, and categories that suggest videos or pictures on subsequent pages. When someone selects a link in any of these pages, the click inadvertently redirects them to another created page containing no pictures or videos but just GACC words and links. The observer team (website owner) creates a revolving door within an inadvertent redirect game that deceives every one that enters their website. However, when a targeted victim enters the team's website, the team can potentially use technology to open a channel, redirecting them into illegal content. Tricky, but an effective way of bringing men down that watches porn.

In recap, external influences coming from observer teams utilizing various deceptive tactics can persuade and direct viewers to inadvertent porn content. Hence, trained, and skilled observers can psychologically influence porn watchers to select GACC as their preferred option. In combining the catalysts of heat and excitement with suggestions, hormones, and neurotransmitters, a greater degree of viewer desire would be the outcome. As the greater degree of desire intensifies, the experience drives the viewer to become addicted on observer directed content. Therefore, they would desire to come back for more after figuring out where the hot spots lie.

Could the members of an observer team consist of spy organizations, GOV contractors, public agents, wives working with girlfriends that want to get rid of their husbands? Absolutely, it could be any team possessing the technology (hardware and software), sending, and listening devices, and skill in verbal persuasion to influence porn viewers.

What about the men that committed suicide (murdered) through psychological torment or humiliation for possessing child porn? Were they under the influence of an observer team before getting busted? Did an observer team psychologically coax the suicide victims along the path of destruction by leading them to illegal content? Could it be that these victims were feeling everything was all right due to the thoughts and feelings generated by the team's persuasion tactics? Aroused males can be subject to behavior modification through suggestion and feeling, especially when neurotransmitters and hormones are involved. Observation teams can even use persuasion power to send suggestible males to seek children in foreign countries like Mexico. The power of suggestion is immensely potent in altering human behavior or getting someone to act unconsciously.

Again, the allowance of GACC places porn viewers that are more susceptible to suggestion at higher risk, especially when covertly observed using deceptive methods. Just like the true story about the store detective, all it takes is a couple of unethical software engineers or GOV contractors to have a good time accessing citizen online porn activity to destroy their lives.

GACC is child exploitation. If we keep allowing GACC within porn, how many more future victims would fall to their demise. We do not need future victims to feel the public humiliation due to observer team influences. Is GACC legal because observer teams can bring men down that watch porn by leading them into illegal content?

Chapter 9: Keep Adult Porn Strictly Adult

Adult entertainment should be strictly free of child related content (GACC) whether through words, categories, links, picture, or videos, but it is not the case. Just place nudity and sex terms in any search engine's query box, and the result will yield numerous websites containing GACC. Evidently the GOV has no intention to step in and eliminate GACC in adult entertainment for some unknown reason, which is shocking. Observation through pornography can uncover that some website owners use GACC to bridge legal content to illegal content. GACC can entice aroused males that stream adult entertainment to become indifferent and captivated with younger female models. Man's innate or genetic sexual attraction for younger females had existed for thousands of years prior to the changes in social laws. So, let us briefly look back in time regarding our ancestry to get a better understanding of previously accepted social behavior.

Humans have an innate or genetic desire to want to have children and families, which is a survival instinct. However, it was within the past one hundred and thirty years that the age of consent changed for the betterment of our social system. This change seemed to be aligned with the progression of making high school mandatory, which is quite interesting. Arguably, this change has benefited our modern-day society by controlling the population, allowing children to build maturity through an elongated family environment, and most important allow our kids to be well-educated citizens in preparation for adulthood and the workplace. Our contemporary educational system has enhanced our scientific knowledge to higher and higher levels of understanding. In developing innovative technology through advanced education, we have improved our lifestyle and can live longer than years past.

Before the age of innovation, the age of consent was much younger for thousands of years, when the world's population was much smaller, and education was limited. During the hundreds and hundreds of years prior to the change, our male ancestors engaged in sexual activity with younger teens, which was very normal behavior. Even though people for the most part lived shorter lives, males engaged in sex with the underage as defined by today's standards. The fact is that males were marrying much younger females back to the days of the early bible. The uneducated of today would describe this ancestry behavior as sick. According to the uneducated, their ancestors were sick, which makes them possess sick blood.

Civil laws regarding the age of consent caused a change in our social behavior and citizens must be totally compliant with these laws. However, the change in laws does not eliminate innate human impulses that lasted for thousands of years. So, can GACC act as a catalyst to unlock those innate urges within our brain that can subconscious lead males to younger females? Males with an innate or genetic induced attraction to younger females may find it difficult to turn away when porn offers GACC to be experienced to the fullest. Hence, the abundance of GACC within porn can drive some males to become fixated on younger females.

We must abolish the games played by website owners that try to entice males to find interest in adolescent females. It is just simply making many GACC illegal within online adult entertainment. The fact is that adult males cannot become sexually interested in young models or underage females, if porn was strictly free of categories, links, words, and pictures referencing children either implied or explicitly.

Simply keep adult entertainment focused on only adult content. New adult entertainment legislation must focus on strictly keeping adult entertainment free of child related categories, words, links, and pictures. It is important that we eliminate GACC from porn before it hurts more of the newer generation that is finding enjoyment in their first amendment rights. We know GACC is one gateway or bridge to illegal porn. The question is, who are the real perverts adding child related words and pictures to adult content? There must be a restructuring of online porn for greater control among those profiting from its business, and OSOMA is the answer.

Part II: A Better Approach to Online Porn

Chapter 10: A Necessitated Approach

Lacking any interest in clicking through its websites, some citizens view internet porn as unfruitful and nonproductive. Bible followers would define it as a rebirth of Sodom and Gomora awaiting Gods destruction. Many devote homemakers and moms would desire it to be abolished from the face of the earth. Dedicated religious men try to avoid it at all costs, but some occasionally fall into its sin. However, there are still millions of accepting viewers achieving a positive experience from flipping through its contents.

In researching porn statistics, it is surprising to uncover the facts regarding the number of individuals that view porn daily. Some individual's desire sessions that last for minutes, while others can experience porn sessions that last for hours. One thing seems certain among active supporters are that they desire to reach a level of satisfaction. The problem is that when millions of aroused enthusiast view page after page of porn, they frequently encounter child content.

The First Amendment of the constitution protects the rights of its citizens to view pornography. However, laws that restrict certain types of porn have created an issue with the GOV excessively monitoring its citizen's. When we read about court cases dealing with illegal porn, we find that the GOV has seemingly added child porn content on the front end and then arrest people that possess it on the backend. It is as if authorities print fake money, entice citizens to buy some on the web at a discount, and then arrest them at the grocery stores when they make food purchases. Many citizens thought the GOV was using taxpayer dollars to find the sources of child porn to eradicate it from the web instead of facilitating its availability. It is confusing and not making much sense.

In reviewing court cases, the GOV methods to combat illegal porn are not wise tax dollars spent. In using these cases, let us put together a hypothetical scenario of the potential methodology utilized. Picture an authoritative agency on the beach digging a sizeable hole in the sand (illegal porn trap), covering it up with a blanket or towel, and then topping it off with sand. What appears is a sandy area like all other spots on the beach, but it is a dangerous hidden hole. Then, the agency sends out men, women, and contractors as observer teams waving the GACC flag to bait and lure beach goes to come over to the hole in hopes of falling in for public humiliation. Does this make sense?

Pondering upon this hypothetical example brings about many questions regarding the true essence of democracy. First, it is unethical for a democratic authority to allow unwarranted games to destroy citizens lives using children as bait. These actions are communistic and inhumane. Second, why are children pieces of meat and manipulative tools used within the fire of porn where sexual pleasure is the objective? This seems clearly unfounded, immoral, exploitive, and evil. The authority's job is to protect all citizens and not obstruct their constitutional rights. However, the authorities are impeding citizens' rights by allowing the use of child baiting tools while viewers are enjoying their freedoms watching adult entertainment. Adult porn should be free of all child related content whether in words or pictures, but it is not.

The GOV has taken an irresponsible approach by not protecting those citizens that enjoy watching adult entertainment in the privacy of their home. They have been leaning toward protecting those citizens that despise porn rather than considering both sides equally. If the GOV focused on sources of illegal content and allowed internet search engines to monitor and control end user content, taxpayers would save millions of dollars. The GOV would also profit from billions of dollars in porn revenue. However, the GOV would rather spend countless taxpayer dollars unproductively by monitoring citizens while impeding their First Amendment rights. There is a better and more cost-effective method to combat the problems of porn and the internet search engines are the answer!

Chapter 11: Out of Sight Out of Mind

A major conflict about the porn industry centers its attention on the rules of social morality versus the law rooted in the constitution. Adversaries see porn as a moral disgrace to our society while supporters view it as an expression of their rights. Homemakers, religious leaders, parent organizations, educators, and anti-porn activists want to eliminate online porn entirely because of its evil influence. Advocates feel citizens have a right to view it at will among other types of freedoms allowed by our constitution. In considering both sides equally, could we keep porn hidden from all general web searches and still provide individuals with their constitutional freedom? The answer is yes by implementing a program called the out of sight out of mind approach (OSOMA). In implementing this approach, the GOV can equitably support both advocates and adversaries of adult entertainment while keeping our children out of porn. In fact, OSOMA is a response to the South Carolina, bill H5414 by deterring adolescence from accessing adult entertainment.

OSOMA will restructure how adult entertainment is going to be available on the internet. First off, there would be a shift of responsibility from the GOV to internet search engines (ISE) and web-hosting companies (WHC) for porn administration, monitoring, and control. Why would the shift to ISE be beneficial? Parent companies of ISE have plenty of cash flow (some have billions), skilled software and hardware personnel, and expertise in developing technology to create a secured login portal to keep the kids out. The GOV spends millions upon millions of taxpayer dollars attempting to enforce illegal porn laws. Yet, we frequently hear from the news and court cases about people possessing its content. This leads to the belief that the GOV is doing an extremely poor job at eliminating it from the web. Why should the taxpayers fork out millions of dollars for porn enforcement when the GOV has failed to annihilate its presence?

Another reason for the shift is that the GOV has failed to criminalize and fine website owners for fraud, abuse, and misrepresentation. Adult website owners liberally use teen and young terms to attract aroused male viewers, deceitfully use inadvertent redirects, label links and categories deceptively, and steer viewers to questionable content. Some website owners even created depraved categories and webpages comprising incest, rape, and bestiality that are criminal offences within our society. The GOV working through OSOMA will prohibit these activities and keep porn authentic and transparent between the viewer and the creator.

Furthermore, the GOV has been negligent in keeping internet porn out of the hands of children. Congressional Bill H5414 stipulates that children between the ages of nine and eleven have experienced online pornography. In this world of technology, our kids can still access pornography even though households engage in internet blocking practices. OSOMA would considerably eliminate adult content on the web and deny underage access to porn by creating a secured login porn portal. A significant outcome is that general searches on the internet for nudity, sex, or pornography would result in zero findings. Parents would no longer have to worry about their kids accessing porn, which would be a benefit to the sanctity of family life. Preteens and teens must be free from the corruption and hazards that porn can inflict upon their lives.

Finally, GOV contractors with access to citizen's online activity have leaked their viewing information out to the public. It would become law that the GOV agencies and contractors could no longer monitor citizen porn activities if streamed within approved search engines. This would create a greater privacy among those that advocate its content and desire total confidentiality.

It is time to let the ISE and WHC take control and responsibility for end user online porn activities. The ISE are the ones delivering content to viewers in the first place from their database of resources. Isn't it the ISE's inventory of resources (accessible database), which has been making them the big bucks? Importantly, the GOV would generate millions of dollars in annual revenue from allowing adult entertainment restructuring through OSOMA. The overall outcome is that the web would be clean and free of all adult entertainment protecting the underage from viewing its contents, which is the most important reason for restructuring porn.

Chapter 12: Putting OSOMA to Action

Under OSOMA, there would be a shift of control and monitoring from the GOV to internet search engines (ISE) for all online adult entertainment. A reason for the shift is that ISE parent companies have plenty of cash flow, software and hardware expertise, and knowledge in controlling queries within their database of sources. Accountability will fall on ISE to locate all porn to a secured login portal where adult entertainment can only be accessible. Alternatively, the ISE can create a separate search engine just for adult entertainment content while leaving their mainstream search engine free of adult entertainment.

ISE would keep porn inside of the secured portal, continually monitor for portal porn leaks, stop, and report illegal porn content, and keep the general web free of adult entertainment. ISE would be required to figure out the features and technical operational specifications using artificial intelligence (AI) as an option. Search tags related to adult entertainment will be regulated and limited, which includes a prohibition of child related wording within porn. ISE would create a specialized department

with a qualified workforce to control and monitor porn activities needed to meet OSOMA objectives.

The GOV would generate millions of dollars in revenue from shifting to this approach. Within OSOMA, the GOV would create general guidelines on how ISE and web hosting companies (WHC) would control, package, and report porn. All ISE, WHC, web browsers, adult entertainment website owners, adult media and streaming services, and adult applications among others would require licensing and certification. Through certification and licensing these sources can house porn content following regulated guidelines. The GOV would fine, shutdown and prosecute unlicensed and non-compliant companies. All child modeling and naturalistic websites would have their own controlled login portal separate from porn and will not be accessible through a general internet search.

ISE and WHC would also be responsible for reporting suspected creators and distributors of illegal porn content to the proper GOV agency. Viewers can also become whistleblowers and receive monetary compensation from search engines or GOV when they come across questionable content. Why not let the porn

viewers become watchdogs because there are millions of eyes involved in porn daily? This approach would leave the GOV free to intensify their efforts by uncovering actual sources of illegal porn.

All adult entertainment enthusiasts desiring entrance to the secured login porn portal must apply to the GOV to obtain a registration number and User ID. The minimum requirements for a viewer to start the application process is to have a valid US driver's license or its equivalent for verification of age, proof of address, and a onetime application fee. The GOV would also charge an annual fee to maintain the applicant records. This would allow the applicant to access adult media, streaming services, and adult applications. Failure to pay the annual charge would force the viewer to re-register and pay another application fee for portal entrance. The GOV would only provide the applicant's registration number and User ID to all licensed ISE's and adult media sources while keeping the applicant's personal information confidential.

Approved viewers using their user ID and number would register with each ISE and create a password to get access to the secured login porn portal. The GOV will

prohibit search engines from asking or obtaining the applicant's personal information. Search engines engaging in this practice will suffer financial penalties and could lose their licenses.

This required porn portal registration would minimize the underage population from accessing porn. High school students that are 18 cannot access porn until after graduation. Legal aged adults providing underage individuals with their login ID's and passwords will be fined and prosecuted. It would also be illegal for an approved applicant to allow someone else to use his or her ID and password for access. Failure to obey this porn portal law would cause a suspension plus a financial penalty.

The GOV would disclose to its citizens which search engines are porn compliant and the ones that are not. The US will attempt to work with foreign-based search engine firms to follow the same standards. All search engines using US based ISE data must become compliant. Foreign ISE's cannot use resources from US based ISE's until certified and licensed. Further, approved ISE cannot allow searchable links to unapproved ISE or web browsers within their database of sources. Application stores cannot contain unlicensed web browser apps. It would also be

illegal for individual website owners to carry any links to unapproved search engines, which will result in financial penalties and prosecution.

Viewers that download questionable content through an approved GOV search engine cannot face financial penalties or prosecution. The GOV approved ISE's would be considered the viewers' safe zone. However, the GOV should mandate that all US citizens must only be conducting adult entertainment queries through licensed portals. Citizens conducting porn searches on unlicensed adult sources should face fines. Underground porn operations either legal or illegal will become a heavily penalized area.

New laws would stipulate that all public companies, federal, state, and local organizations, schools, universities, libraries, and nonprofit agencies could only use GOV approved search engines on all devises with blocked access to the porn portal. Private LLC and corporations using the internet must only allow GOV approved search engines on all work devises but can allow access to the secured porn portal if desired.

Satisfaction will reach the hearts of homemakers, religious groups, and anti-porn activists because searches

for nudity, sex, or porn on the internet will return zero findings. Further, underage individuals will have an extremely hard time accessing porn content, which can help them focus on important things like education, family activities, school functions, and sports. Many teenagers have fallen victim to porn at a young age because of poor GOV control and the ease of obtaining porn on the internet. Many teens have suffered porn addiction right into adulthood. The time is now to give adult entertainment back to those citizens that enjoy watching it in the privacy of their home through a secure login portal while preventing the underage population from viewing its contents.

Chapter 13: GOV Revenue Sources

Porn is an expanding worldwide multibillion dollar industry with millions of searches conducted daily by enthusiasts. ISE's are a major gateway to access porn content on the web. So, why should taxpayer dollars have to pay for the control and monitoring of porn when ISE's are making the big bucks? It is about time that the GOV allowed the ISE's and web hosting companies (WHC) to take control of end user porn activity. In shifting control, there would be billions of dollars of GOV revenue generated over time from fees and taxes, plus countless savings in taxpayer dollars.

The most significant adult entertainment revenue source would come from the mature viewing population. The GOV would charge an initial application fee for individuals wanting to access porn through the secured login porn portal. Adult entertainment viewers would also pay an additional annual tax to maintain their privately held credentials on file with the GOV. The benefit to citizens paying fees and taxes is that the burden of illegal content falls on ISE's, WHC, and websites owners. Legal adult aged citizens providing underage individuals with

their login ID's and passwords will face fines and prosecution. Also, adults lending their User ID, password, or registration number will be fined and suspended from the use of the portal.

ISE's, WHC, web browsers, adult entertainment websites, adult media and streaming services, and adult applications (among others) are required to pay licensing fees and annual taxes. All foreign-based search engines that carry porn content created by US companies must also obtain a license, pay fees, and annual taxes. US search engines that do not want to carry porn will not have to have a license. However, if nudity, sex, or pornography arises within an unlicensed search engine, there will be financial penalties.

All websites having any implicit or explicit nudity, sex, or pornography on their website must go through a GOV certification process and obtain a license with applicable fees and annual taxes. Websites such as adult dating services with sexual encounters, sex story sites, adult toy and video online stores, porn services, sex communication sites, all sites containing sexual content outside of medicine would pay licensing fees and annual taxes.

Periodic audits of ISE, WHC, and website owners would ensure compliance with GOV certification standards. Failure to maintain proper internal control and monitoring after certification could cause executive monetary penalties, corporate fines, and potential loss of a license. These actions would tighten up general searches inside and outside of the secured porn portal. The GOV would also fine, shutdown, and prosecute unlicensed firms and owners.

ISE and WHC must attempt to shut down and immediately report suspected creators and distributors of illegal porn content to the proper GOV agency. Failure to disclose questionable sources of illegal porn can lead to fines and loss of certification. Millions of porn viewers can also be the watchdogs and receive compensation from the search engines when they disclose questionable content.

All child modeling websites and naturalistic sites (with kids) must have their own controlled login portal separate from porn that will not be accessible through a general internet search. This content is sensitive and must not mix with adult entertainment. These websites will also require certification licensing fees and annual taxes.

In recap, search engines, web-hosting firms, browsers, and website owners must be the ones to take on the responsibility for adult content. They must suffer financial penalties for not maintaining certification standards inside and outside of the secured porn portal. The reason is that these companies are profiting heavily from internet activities, which porn is a source. Why should the taxpayer have to pay for porn monitoring and control? Finally, the revenue generated from sources of porn and the taxpayer's savings will add a chunk of money in the GOV's pocket.

Chapter 14: Recapping OSOMA

There needs to be a fair compromise between the adversaries and advocates of pornography in America while keeping our children locked out of all adult entertainment. The government's ineffectiveness to eradicate GACC, illegal porn, website owner fraud and deception, and immoral categories must change through restructuring. In restructuring, internet search engines and web hosting companies would take total control of end-user porn enforcement. In using OSOMA, the GOV would generate billions of dollars in adult entertainment revenues over time through certification, licensing, annual fees, and financial penalties.

Each GOV approved search engine would create a login portal that would contain all searchable adult entertainment. ISE can create a distinct adult entertainment search engine while keeping their principal search engine clear of nudity, sex, and pornography. In implementing OSOMA, all general internet searches for nudity, sex, or pornography will yield zero findings. To access the secured porn portal, adults would have to register with the GOV using a driver's license (or equivalent) and provide address verification. The required registration would significantly reduce underage access to pornography. All child modeling and naturalistic websites would have their own controlled login portal separate from porn.

Accountability would fall upon the search engines and web-hosting companies to keep porn inside of the secured portal, continually monitor for portal porn leaks, stop access of illegal porn content, and keep the general web searches free of adult entertainment. The ISE would inform the GOV relating to creators and developers of illegal porn. The GOV also would audit and fine search engine and hosting companies that are non-compliant with established standards. Finally, the GOV would publicly make available a list of approved and unlicensed search engines for the viewing audience.

In being compliant, porn viewers, search activities will not be monitored and kept private from GOV personnel and contractors. This would severely reduce the extensive leaking of porn viewer's personal information that has been going on for years by unethical GOV contractors. Porn supporters can also become whistleblowers or watchdogs and receive compensation from the search engine when they come across questionable content.

The result of restructuring through OSOMA would eliminate all nudity and porn from all internet searches, allow for a secure adult entertainment portal, mandate porn addiction ads in portals, eliminate underage porn access, eradicate GACC and illegal porn, allow for whistleblowing activities, eliminate rape and incest categories, save the taxpayer millions of dollars, and preserve lives, careers, reputation, and families.

Part III: Protect Our Children

Chapter 15: Summary Bill SC H5414

This chapter evaluates the South Carolina Bill H5414 (123rd General Assembly) with subsequent personal comments. Bill H5414 focuses on the essential need to take measures in protecting minors from internet pornography, which is a public health hazard. The Bill also expresses a need to stop child and woman exploitation in pornography.

Bill: The members of the assembly recognize that the average age of exposure to pornography is now between the ages of nine and eleven years old. Because of the advances of technology and global accessibility, minors have been accessing mainstream (hardcore) pornography.

Comments: The GOV has failed to unearth a means of protecting our minors from gaining access to adult entertainment on the web. Therefore, it is essential for restructuring online pornography to protect child exploitation (GACC) within its content while protecting child access by using a secured login portal within each internet search engine.

Bill: The assembly shows that sex traffickers have been using victims to make pornography material that is often violent in nature without the victim's approval. Porn viewers streaming through adult content cannot discern if victim's performances were consensual or exploitive in nature.

Comments: When active porn enthusiasts become enticed, mesmerized, and excited through hormones and triggered neurotransmitters, porn of all types can become attractive and accepting. Therefore, it can be hard for porn viewers to discern exploitative porn activities. Additionally, some porn websites and channels label categories as teen abuse, which should be made illegal.

Bill: The assembly states that pornography treats women and children as objects and depicts violence, rape, and abuse as if these acts were harmless. This increases the risk of normalizing these deplorable activities.

Comments: Gray area child content (GACC) has been in porn for years that uses children as pieces of bait and sexual objects with no government intervention. GACC comprise child related words, categories, links, and visual depictions that are clearly positioned within adult content where millions of aroused viewers are seeking sexual satisfaction. GACC exploits children either implied or explicitly among its countless pages. In addition, child transition pages can persuade aroused males to look at children as sexual objects. Website owners also create categories such as incest, rape, and bestiality that are criminal offences within our society and use women and children in an exploitive manner. Minors uncovering this material online may believe that incest and even rape are not deviant social behaviors. This twisted distortion may lead teenagers into acting it out on siblings and innocent victims.

Bill: The assembly shows that early exposure of pornography to teenagers and prepubescent children contributes to the hyper-sexualization of these individuals. The effect can lead children to low self-esteem, body image disorders, an increase in problematic sexual activity, and an increased desire among adolescents to engage in risky sexual behavior. Pornography often serves as sex education and informs the sexual templates of teenagers and children.

Comments: Online porn creates a fabricated environment of sexual lust and desire that submerges a teenager's mind away from the truth about family, marriage, and fidelity. Depending on the level of exposure, porn can rewire a teenager's brain, inhibiting them from developing into a responsible adult. Porn can also influence a child's social and personal well-being, create academic problems, and cause withdrawals from school activities.

Bill: The assembly shows that it is critical to recognize the malicious effect that pornography has on society when distributed carelessly over the internet without regard for the disturbing and lasting effects that it can cause.

Comments: A major problem with internet porn is the ease of access at little or no cost, which can lead to addiction. An addiction could emerge when the craving to keep watching porn overcomes the ability to stop. Addiction could also occur at a point where viewing porn takes priority over employment, important household duties, family, and personal relationships. The uncontrollable beast of porn must be confined and regulated. Additionally, dependency ads must be required in porn to make viewers aware of addiction.

Bill: The members of the General Assembly recognize that pornography is creating a public health crisis and action must be taken to address pornography in a manner like public health regulation used in the past to combat issues like smoking, lead poisoning, and HIV/AIDS. Whereas, addressing pornography must be done systemically by enacting policies that would help to prevent exposure and addiction, educate individuals on its harmful effects, and develop recovery plans while holding providers accountable.

Comments: OSOMA as a plan of action would eliminate adult content on the web and deny underage access to porn by creating a secured login porn portal. A significant outcome achieved is that general searches on the internet for nudity, sex, or pornography would result in zero findings. Parents would no longer have to worry about their kids getting access to porn, which would be a benefit to the sanctity of family life. Preteens and teens must be free from the corruption and hazards that porn can inflict upon their lives.

In recap, the GOV has stepped forward through this bill in realizing that underage access to porn is damaging to our society and families. Yet, the GOV up to this point has failed in their duty to develop a universal plan to protect the innocent lives of our youth from the destructive elements of porn. Internet search engines can be part of that universal plan for establishing secured porn login portals that require age verification. There is a better way to keep porn closed out of the lives of minors, and OSOMA could be that universal plan.

Chapter 16: Protect Children from Porn

The internet is extraordinarily strong educational tool full of information, resources, and knowledge that our children can use to advance our society. Our kids deserve a chance to learn and grow through the internet while avoiding the dark cloud of pornography looming within its cavity. It is time to set fire to Sodom and Gomorrah and send it to a hidden place on the internet that is absent from the eyes and minds of our children. Using the out of sight, out of mind approach (OSOMA), we can prevent pornography from obstructing our children's minds, which can lead them to a much fuller and happier life.

The problem with most porn is that it is free, uncontrollable, and easily accessible to teenagers even though parents may attempt to block it out. It is sad to see young teenagers that have witnessed the dark cloud of uncontrolled nudity, sex, and pornography on the internet. Children as early as the age of nine have embraced sexuality on the web. Depending on the level of exposure, porn can rewire a teenager's brain preventing them from evolving into a responsible adult.

Porn can affect a child's social and personal well-being, create academic problems, and pull kids away from the important periods of child growth. Porn can also influence a teen's sexual gender by creating attractions through sight and sounds that if porn were absent, the change would be lacking. Online porn can facilitate sex among our underage teens that can lead into disease and unwanted pregnancy. It is devastating when children in high school become pregnant because of the influence of porn.

Online porn creates a fictitious environment of sexual lust and desire that submerges a teenager's mind away from the reality of life. Some teenagers witnessing sex online desire to be part of that experience filled with pleasure and excitement. Porn vultures seek naive young girls to pose nude in photographs or videos for money. Legal aged teenagers that fall prey to porn vultures may end up exposed on websites engaged in sexual acts for the world to witness. Many teenagers have regretted their porn decision, realizing that it was foolish and wrong.

It is time to create a secured login porn portal that can be accessible to adults while keeping our kids locked out. We must stop the uncontrollable spread of porn to our young citizens so they may focus on more of the quality things in life, like studies, sports, school, and family. We must stop this beast before our next generation develops into a group of immoral citizens. The GOV failed to take initiative and responsibility for controlling pornography on the internet. However, under the proposed OSOMA, important changes can take place to protect our youth. OSOMA will minimize porn from our children's world, so they can grow up focusing on the important things in life.

Chapter 17: Child Rape and Incest

Incest and rape are two controversial pornography categories that are easily accessible by conducting a search through the internet. Committing incest and rape are criminal offenses in America that are prosecutable under federal and state law. It is odd that our regulators would allow words, pictures, and videos relating to these topics available through an online porn search. A potential reason could be that videos and pictures found under these categories are presumably fake.

Incestuous relationships and scenes of rape occur within movie productions and TV series with limited sexual content. However, there are hundreds of explicit sexual rape and incest videos found online and in adult bookstores, which is a significant difference than a few screenplay movies. Both categories in adult entertainment tend to exploit women and children as sexual objects. It is disconcerting to realize that viewers are getting sexual satisfaction from watching this material.

There are many videos and pictures within the porn market labeled as incest. Porn website owners desire to create an impression in the viewer's mind that incest is an acceptable and permissible act. These website owners create various categories such as father-daughter, father-son, mother-son, and mother-daughter, just to name a few. Within some incest websites, there are real family members involved in sexual encounters such as twins engaged in erotic activity. However, the production of some of these incestuous videos is within countries that allow it. In some country's incest is a very permissible act allowed by law unlike the US. Therefore, the incestuous activities undergone by these family members are legal to produce in their country, but it is still illegal sex in the US.

Now imagine a picture of a parent with underage children in the household sitting on their computer in a home office engaged in incestuous porn on the internet. What happens if the parent's attachment to incest becomes serious? Could one of their children be in jeopardy of losing their innocence because of desire and pleasure created by this online material? What is a simple route for a parent to take when incest porn becomes a real craving? What happens when a close relative is hooked on this type of porn like an uncle, grandparent, or cousin and encounters your children regularly? Relatives seem to be a prime predator for incest and rape of familiar children, which are an easy target.

Rape is an illegal sexual act that involves the use of force against the will of a person which could occur when a person is conscious, unconscious, drugged, or intoxicated. Rape also entails an adult having sex with a minor, either forced or even consensual. Rape videos can psychologically influence vulnerable individuals to experience deep pleasure or become infatuated in watching individuals force themselves on others. Can you image porn addicts getting sexual gratification from watching rape within adult websites? It is surprising that the GOV has not stepped in and banned words, categories, pictures, or videos relating to this implied violent content.

What would be the mental impact of a minor that finds online rape and incest videos thinking they are real? Since the GOV failed in providing a universal plan to isolate minors from online porn, minors pose an exposure risk. Minors finding this material online may believe that incest and rape are not deviant behaviors. This created distortion may lead teenagers into acting it out on siblings and innocent victims. They may force themselves on peers to get satisfaction. Further, it could damage them for life depending upon the impression left within their minds.

Many porn dwellers may find rape and incest videos to be highly offensive, questionable, and disturbing. However, there is some acceptance of incest and rape related topics among porn viewers within the shell of porn. The reason could be that many porn viewers coming across these categories know that the videos are lacking in authenticity, more so rape than incest. However, extended viewing of rape videos might have a psychological effect on an addicted porn viewer. It is possible that some viewers might perceive these videos as training for future activities.

It is the moral duty of our GOV to prohibit incest and rape categories, words, links, and videos within porn. Porn viewers can undergo an influence driven by curiosity to explore its topics with an open mind, especially minors that are exposed to its content. These videos could create fantasies that turn into reality. This type of adult entertainment must be stopped.

Chapter 18: Protect Kids Grade One

Clergy supervising a summer camp in upstate New York molested my brother in the second and third grade. Since we are a dedicated family to the faith, my dad tried to avoid pursuing prosecution for these incidences. He kept it quiet not to alarm the parishioners and not put disfavor upon his faith. Therefore, my brother had nowhere to go regarding these rape incidences, which left him emotionally injured. If he had someone to contact for support outside of the family, his quality of life might have improved upon reaching adulthood. All minors need a source outside of the family where they can talk about incidences that occur in their life regarding inappropriate touching or rape. But how can a child have knowledge if our education system does not train them starting grade one?

There is a necessity for mandated sexual abuse training for students in primary and secondary education across the country. All students from first grade to their senior year in high school should undergo documented sexual abuse training annually. Implementing this course of action would allow each child an opportunity to learn personal protection and have a place to report sexual abuse other than within their home. Standardized training in sexual abuse throughout all our nation's schools would achieve an extremely high student penetration rate. Some of us encountered child abuse growing up and had no place to go like myself. Today, our children need protection using new standards in sexual abuse guidance provided by our educational system.

Training can take place at home with the parents or in schools by a trained psychologist. This program would require all schools have on staff at least one psychologist trained in child abuse. The student sexual abuse training can cover areas like appropriate and inappropriate touching, respecting others, awareness of strangers, keeping together, and reporting abuse. Standardized forms that are signed by parents, teachers, school psychologists, and the student can be used throughout the US.

The school will provide parents with training material, if they want to train their kids at home. Home schooled kids must train at a nearby school away from their guardians. The student and school must sign off stating that training has been adequately completed.

Parents training their child at home must submit the appropriate signed documentation to the school. The homeroom teacher or psychologist with the student would review and sign the documentation once it arrives at the school. Testing will be the assessment used to ensure that the students have understood the required material. Failing the test would require retraining at the student's school. Mandatory testing for home schooled students would take place at a nearby school.

Critical areas within training can include behavior with others and self, awareness of strangers, keeping together in pairs or groups, and not being fearful to reporting incidences. This program will also train our school-age children from first grade to show respect of others and self. Students will also train on becoming perceptive and vigilant within their surrounding environment for suspicious people in parks, neighborhoods, school grounds, and other locations. During training, students will learn the importance of reporting incidences immediately to the school psychologist or teacher.

Starting grade seven and each year following, it would be mandatory for students to go through a lecture series concerning mob rings and human trafficking. Students will also learn the importance of reporting other classmates that are involved in prostitution or had contacts with traffickers.

In recap, children need to start at a young age to understand how to protect themselves from abuse. My brother had no one to turn to for help when he encountered sexual abuse early in life. Through this program, students will learn the urgency and necessity of reporting incidences to a teacher or school psychologist immediately. Our young students trained and conditioned in sexual abuse early in life will lead them into proper human behaviors right into college and on to the workplace.

Chapter 19: Porn and Family

Today, it is unbelievable what statistics reveal about the number of households that are watching online adult entertainment regularly. Online pornography in the US has gotten way out of control and is crumbling the family unit into pieces. A congressional bill labels porn as a sexual poison that is causing a social health crisis and destroying individual, marriages, and families. Former president Bush wrote that porn has a devastating impact on marriages, families, and children.

Porn is impacting our family structure by promoting page after page of uncontrollable sexual pleasure leading good marriages into infidelity. Porn has taken married people away from that special sexual bond and cast it aside as a worthless institution. It is no wonder why marriages are at an all-time low and single parenting is a way of life.

Children are the centerpiece of a solid and happy marriage. Parents that split apart end up hurting our children. Kids need a healthy environment with two nurturing parents to help them grow successfully into this complex world. How can a stable marriage exist unless there is a solid commitment within the relationship among its members? The reality is that porn is one of the suspected culprits splitting families apart.

Children are our future and need proper nurturing to instill good family and social values. Without the firm family foundation and education through the growing years, a child's ethics will decrease. The concept of a family is not porn based but quite the opposite. However, underage teenagers that view porn can develop misconceptions about relationships.

Porn can influence our young into thinking that it is a natural way of living when it corrodes the family unit. We must preserve the important values within the minds of our children and focus their thoughts on the importance of education, family, and fidelity. Some of our college students are making money through porn as models when they should study for their careers and think about raising a family.

The growth of Sodom and Gomorrah is taking our young adults away from the ideas of the family structure, and the GOV seems to lack any interest. If we do not take control of this porn beast, it will eat us alive.

Part IV: Final Chapters

Chapter 20: The Conclusion

Child exploitation has been occurring for many years in pornography because of our government's lack of intentional commitment. First, The GOV was neglectful to create a better means of protecting our minors from gaining access to online pornography. South Carolina bill H5414 states that between the ages of nine and eleven, children are viewing online pornography. Porn can rewire a teenager's brain to think in a distorted manner by corrupting their perception regarding family, marriage, morality, and fidelity.

Second, the government has been allowing GACC in porn, which is clearly child exploitation. Children are not pieces of meat or manipulative tools to use within the fire of porn where sexual pleasure is the objective. GACC leads porn viewers to feel indifferent about the true meaning of words and categories related to children like youth, teen, lolita, and barely legal that appear frequently. GACC influences aroused males to treat children as sexual objects. By not placing bans on GACC, the GOV is consenting that viewers should feel perfectly normal selecting child related words, pictures, and categories in porn.

Porn is an uncontainable multibillion dollar industry deficient in adequate regulation to criminalize and fine website owners for fraud, misrepresentation, and child exploitation. Porn website owners freely use child related material to entice viewers, deceitfully optimize inadvertent redirects, label misleadingly, and even attempt to steer viewers to illegal content. Some website owners produce webpages containing categories such as incest, rape, and bestiality that are criminal offences within our society. These owners are treating women and children as sexual objects.

The solution is OSOMA, which is an innovative approach that mandates the creation of a secured login portal for all online adult entertainment. This secured portal would permanently lock out minor access because of the verification of age and address requirements. In using OSOMA, an internet search for topics related to nudity, sex, or pornography would result in zero findings. OSOMA is the answer that would keep the internet a very safe and clean environment for all ages to appreciate the facts, data, statistics, information, and knowledge that it possesses. Now it is time to confine and control the porn beast while we have a chance before it destroys American as a nation.

Chapter 21: Forethought

The spirit of this work is to offer a solution to the South Carolina Bill H5414 regarding the abuse of children and women in pornography and the dangers of child exposure to online pornography. It is in great hope that this work gets into the hands of homemakers, religious leaders, porn adversaries, and judicial decision makers to help change the scope and direction of pornography in America. It is with strong optimism that after publication of this work changes may take place in the future that may outdate some of its contents. OSOMA is a system. However, no system is infallible and there are always holes found in it that will need repairs. Still, a system in place is better than no system.